From beatific bluebirds to the blunt finality of a spent gun, Lee Varon expertly couples the beauty and allure of nature with the sting of tragedy. A truly unique collection with lush imagery, artfully tarnished with heartbreak.

—Doug Holder, Editor *Ibbetson Street Press*, author of *Last Night At The Wursthaus*

Lee Varon's poems take us to the shooting of her grandfather in 1936. The images like "a blush that turned to blood," are breathtaking. At first it is a family story, but as you examine it further, the views of prejudice in the community are jaw-dropping, yet amazingly relevant to today's issues. Her grandmother, Virginia Marie, navigates life with pride and loyalty, yet fear and bigotry, highlighting the complexity of human nature.

—Jean Flanagan, author of *Black Lightning*

"When you returned / from your father's funeral / smell of the mill / like pinking shears, / cut through your lungs." So insists the speaker of Lee Varon's *Shot in the Head*, addressing her grandmother as she relives her grandparents' tragic connection, marred by infidelity and revenge. These poems, sharpened on the whetstone of Varon's grandmother's genteel deprivations, bigotry, and disappointment, cut with the same keen edge. It's a stunning collection, from start to finish.

—Tom Daley, author of *House You Cannot Reach*

FIRST PLACE ♦ POETRY COLLECTION

Shot In The Head

LEE VARON

SUNSHOT PRESS

FIRST PLACE • 2017 SUNSHOT BOOK AWARD™ FOR POETRY

Shot In The Head
© 2017 Lee Varon

Published 2018 by Sunshot Press, an imprint of *New Millennium Writings*.

EDITOR-IN-CHIEF
Alexis Williams Carr

ASSOCIATE PUBLISHER | COVER & BOOK DESIGN
Brent Carr

CONSULTING EDITOR EMERITUS
Don Williams

CONTRIBUTING EDITORS AND SUPPORT
*Laura Still, Rebecca Moody, Linda Parsons,
Chloe Hanson, Joseph Mooradian, and others*

3   5   7   9   10   8   6   4   2
ISBN: 978-1-944977-22-1 (Paperback)
ISBN: 978-1-944977-19-1 (Hardcover)
ISBN: 978-1-944977-35-1 (Ebook)

All rights reserved, unless otherwise noted. Except for brief quotations in critical articles or reviews, no part of this publication may be reproduced, copied, transmitted, or distributed, in any way, without written permission from the publisher.

www.sunshots.org
www.musepaper.org
www.newmillenniumwritings.org

SUNSHOT⊙PRESS

New Millennium WRITINGS

In memory of my grandparents:

Marie Maxwell McElroy 1899—1985
Edwin Miller McElroy 1898—1943

PUBLICATION ACKNOWLEDGMENTS

The author would like to thank the editors of the following journals where these poems first appeared, sometimes in earlier versions, under different titles.

Atlanta Review: "Not Much Different"

Bagels with the Bards Anthology: "After Your Argument with my Father"

Cottonwood Magazine: "Edwin's Brother"

Constellations Anthology #7: "Talking," "Stories"

Euphony: "Shot In The Head," "I Wanted To Know," "Edwin," "All Of Something," "You Learned The News"

Fox Chase Review: "Millionaire's Son Shot"

Ibbetson Street: "We Sat Every Night," "After"

Inscape: "Samplar: Betrayal"

Muddy River Review: "Vacation Photo"

OVS Magazine: "Confederate Fantasy"

Oxford Magazine: "Grandmother Goes to Hollywood"

Schuylkill Valley Journal: "You Married Him Anyhow"

The Somerville Times: "You And Stonewall Jackson"

The Round: "1959 With My Grandmother"

Westview: "The Last Time I See Her"

Tampa Review: "Perpetual Care"

Wilderness House Literary Review: "Blister"

Words And Images Journal: "Somehow"

◆

The following poems were published in a 2017 collection entitled "Affairs Run in the Family" by **Finishing Line Press**:

"Affairs Run In The Family"
"After"
"Another Ending"
"Battlefield"
"Blister"
"Caramel Cake, Burnt Sugar Icing"
"Confederate Fantasy"
"Court"
"I Imagine"
"McElroy Chevrolet Sales Corp."
"Meditations on Death"
"Not Much Different"
"Restless With The Dream Of Rest"
"Secrets"
"That Jew"
"To My Grandfather's Lover"
"Trash"
"Uncle"
"Vacation Photo"
"We Sat Every Night"
"With Grandmother At Mother's Funeral"

◆

Parts of the italicized phrases in "Battlefield" are credited to *Bravest Surrender; a Petersburg Patchwork* by Catherine Copeland.

Copeland, Catherine, and P. Hairston Seawell. *Bravest Surrender; a Petersburg Patchwork*. Richmond, VA: Press of Whittet & Shepperson, 1961.

◆

Many thanks to my fellow poets, Jean Flanagan and Tom Daley, for their support and endorsement of this work.

CONTENTS

publication acknowledgments | vi
preface | x
Millionaire's Son Shot | 2

I

Grandmother Goes to Hollywood | 6
Grandmother Learned The News | 7
Battlefield | 8
You Married Him Anyhow | 10
Shot In The Head | 12
Restless with the Dream of Rest | 13
McElroy Chevrolet Sales Corp. Showing Postponed | 14
Secrets | 15
To My Grandfather's Lover | 16
Edwin's Brother | 17
Court | 18
I Imagine | 20
Money | 22
Another Ending | 23

II

Blister | 26
That Jew | 29
Somehow | 30
Gossip | 31
What I Forgot to Tell You After
  the Argument with My Father | 32

Uncle | 33
Her Sister's Regrets | 34
Caramel Cake, Burnt Sugar Icing | 36
Confederate Fantasy | 38
We Sat Every Night | 40
Not Much Different | 42
Fear is a Face Without Features | 43
Trash | 44
With Grandmother at My Mother's Funeral | 45
Food and Flowers, Memorial | 46
You Forgive Them | 47

III

Stories | 50
Affairs Run in the Family | 51
Vacation Photo | 52
Samplar: Betrayal | 53
After | 54
Escape | 55
You and Stonewall Jackson | 56
Talking | 58
The Last Time I See Her | 59
Meditations on Death | 61
Perpetual Care | 62
Together | 63

ABOUT THE AUTHOR | 65
SUNSHOT PRESS | 66

Preface

Shot In The Head focuses on a piece of history that reverberated throughout my life. Many of the poems refer to the 1936 shooting of my grandfather, Edwin McElroy. He was shot in the head by the husband of his lover, which resulted in my grandfather's partial paralysis. There was a trial in which the defendant, prominent local businessman J.J. Harding, was acquitted. My grandfather died several years later at the age of forty-two.

This dramatic event must have colored my grandmother's lifelong distrust of others.

One of five children born in Marietta, Georgia, my grandmother came from Scotch-Irish descendants. She described her father as "an inventor," but I was never quite sure what he invented. Her mother died when she was ten and her father became a 7th Day Adventist, sold everything and sent his children to an Adventist boarding school, which my grandmother hated. When she turned eighteen, alone and penniless, my grandmother made her way out to California, found a job in a real estate company and married the boss's son, my grandfather Edwin, who was originally also from the south. Together the couple moved to Virginia, settling in Petersburg. The couple had two children—my mother and uncle. Both died untimely deaths—my uncle when he was only 18 and my mother at age 48.

Life should have been perfect, but then one fatal night my grandfather was shot in the arms of his lover.

The tragedy of my grandfather's shooting and early death was soon followed by what my grandmother deemed another tragedy. Her only daughter eloped with a Jewish boy she'd met in college. My grandmother was steeped in the racism of the south but her xenophobia was far-reaching and included Jews and Catholics as well as blacks. My grandmother showered affection on me; despite lamenting that I was not born "all of something" (meaning racially "pure").

Although she harbored a lifelong hatred of my father and never visited us up north, my grandmother was happy to have me spend summers with her. I had a difficult relationship with my father and came to see my grandmother as an ally.

While I cherished my grandmother's attention, I became increasingly aware of, and troubled by, the overt racism I saw during my visits with her. I still recall drinking fountains labeled *Whites Only* and the sign in our favorite restaurant: *No Colored Allowed*. When I asked my grandmother about these signs she always told me that "colored people" preferred to stay with their own kind. As if their exclusion was a choice. I argued with her, I pushed back against her views, and she attributed my argumentativeness to my Jewish side—something I couldn't help. It was an unfortunate reality she did her best to ignore.

Yet despite our friction, we always remained close. As one of the last poems in this collection reads: *we laugh as we always did / as if no one ever left anyone.*

I argued with my grandmother but I could have done more. I knew I wouldn't do anything like the twelve-year-old, Janie Miller, who brought water to the freedom fighters choking by their fire-bombed bus. It brings to mind the question in the poem, "We Sat Every Night": *Was I too chicken to have my family / run out of town like Janie's?*

I wondered, was I too chicken to risk losing my grandmother's love?

Poems often seek to understand something more deeply, and many of the poems here are my effort to understand this proud, deeply flawed woman who was so central to my life. *Shot In The Head* began as a book about a tragic incident, but as I wrote, it became less about this one violent event and more about grappling with the moral paradox of a grandmother who was steeped in bigotry and intolerance, and yet who loved me and whom I loved.

—Lee Varon

Millionaire's Son Shot

The Richmond Times, May, 1936

I

Better if he had died
that night at the farmhouse?

I have heirlooms:
quilted satin trimmed with blue velvet,
brilliant cut diamonds,
turquoise cufflinks shot through
with black veins.

But what seeps into my bones
is the story of a marriage:
it began with bluebirds among the crepe myrtle
nearly ended with the smell of gunshot.

II

Grandmother
dreamed she'd be an extra in the movies —
her image on a matchbook wearing a beret
smiling for the camera
but ended up as the main attraction —
the scorned wife
they all came to see at the courthouse.
In her pocket —
crushed magnolias.

III

Grandfather, with his three-piece suit
his easy smile—
I wanted to be
the girl in the photo
he had his arm draped over,
the daughter
he let drive his new cars,

and surprised
with cinnamon candies,
the one who gave him a sip
of water after he was shot.

IV

I never laid eyes on her,
the woman he was shot holding,
her red hair
clotted with blood.

I wanted to be the air
between them,
a wedge of stars.

I

Grandmother Goes to Hollywood

At eighteen you left chickens
scratching in the dust
of Alpharetta;
walked to the train station,
your high-laced boots
froze to your feet.
You had to cut them off.

In L. A.
you kept your mother's picture
folded in your suitcase,
wanted her to be with you
when you were discovered—
her hair so long she sat on it,
her skin as pale
as moon sheen.

Grandmother Learned The News

You were at your father's funeral
in Marietta,
you came home
the train stopped—
hiss of steam
smell of rubber mill
drifting on a hot summer night.

Still in your mourning clothes—
black stockings,
straight seams,
your lawyer met you with the news:
Your husband shot
with *that* woman,
the redhead with bold green eyes.

Magnolias were opening
with their cream colored
edge of pink lace,
fireflies scattered—
and you were almost a widow.

You helped your husband home
paralyzed on his left side,
taught him to use a spoon
hold a pen
almost write
his name.

I wasn't born yet
I wasn't your granddaughter.

Battlefield

FOR MY GRANDMOTHER

The battle of the crater, part of the Siege of Petersburg, took place on July 30, 1864. Grant considered the assault the "saddest affair I have witnessed in the war."*

There was the smell at first—
too much cinnamon,
brandy spilled on honeysuckle.
Then, you brushed off his coat
to place in the cedar chest for winter,
saw the red hair
glinting

They say it was a war of nerves
The Confederates could hear them digging,
but failed to locate the tunnel

No one at his car dealership
had red hair
shot through with gold

A tunnel over 500 feet long,
mined with four tons of black powder

At night sinister fireflies
hovered in the wisteria

It was a hot breathless night…
The very air itself waited…and waited

You went alone to your father's funeral
just to pay respects

A hot sultry night. Suddenly a terrific explosion
tore through the silence,
sending up a giant cloud of smoke.
It descended,
bearing in the flames
the bodies of men
nearly six thousand

The bullet split in two
part coming through his left temple
part embedded in his brain

It slashed a great crater in the earth
…filled with screaming, dying men

If Lieutenant Douty and Sergeant Reese
hadn't volunteered to crawl back in the tunnel
and relight the fuse
the crater would not exist,

if you hadn't gone to your father's funeral
your husband would have come home,
eaten his chicken dinner,
sat down with the children
and played dominoes.

*Parts of the italicized phrases in "Battlefield" are credited to *Bravest Surrender; a Petersburg Patchwork* by Catherine Copeland.

You Married Him Anyhow

Snapdragons and Sweet William
bloomed along the house
on Sycamore Street,
night came
the screen door slammed.
You hadn't shared a bed
with him for years.

The maid, Daisy,
turned down the sheets
left a glass of warm milk
beside your bed.

For a long time you'd smelled
crushed tobacco,
cinnamon
in his pockets
when he returned from work.
Brandy
when he came home late.

The children worshipped him —
he let them drive a Chevrolet
the color of cream,
the one in the dealership window.
He gave the girl a pony
the boy, two dogs.

Everyone adored him—
he let them buy on credit,
Miss Cleo Paton once remarked:
*he was too handsome
to be married.*

You married him anyhow;
You wanted the brilliant cut
diamond, the house
with the breezy parlor,
tang of Sweet William in the flower beds,
Spanish tiles.

When you returned
from your father's funeral
smell of the mill
like pinking shears,
cut through your lungs
as you breathed in the news:
Your husband shot
by his lover's husband.

You straightened the seams
of your black stockings,
went straight to the hospital.
No need to remove your
black felt hat,
its long pin stabbing
your auburn hair.

Shot In The Head

On the wooden swing
you pushed her,
took off her yellow dress slowly,
delicately, like peeling a plum.

Then a fusillade of shots
a fragment raced through your temple
caromed off the iron fence,
another embedded in the pallid sulcus
of your brain.

After the shot
your eyes opened in the hospital
secret shattered by the split bullet—
your nights with your lover—

but your eyes didn't open
on her green eyes
on a fluttering of hope
on tomorrow—

but on your wife's eyes
her anger spilling
like syrup
into the black of night,
fireflies going off
to death's porch.

Restless with the Dream of Rest

Before he was shot
Grandfather wanted his father
to sign the dealership over—
yearned for his name alone on the title.
Now it's too late.

Woods aglow with redbuds,
lambent light in mirror.
He reaches to touch his temple
gnarled with scars—
red, blue, raised.

At St. Paul's they preach
sermons against adultery.

He watches sun gleam on
birds splash
and dreams
of nights with his lover.

Barely able to speak,
he drags his left leg behind him
like a dead animal,

remembers taking
the cream-colored Chevrolet,
driving beside her
to the theater with its high
blue ceiling.

McElroy Chevrolet Sales Corp. Showing Postponed

On the corner of Union Street
his Chevrolet dealership
is empty.

A notice in the window: *The Spring Showing
has been postponed from May 20th
to July 1st.*

It gives no reason.
A wasp nest has settled
under the rafters.

Secrets

The children are happy
to have their daddy home.
They are helping me type a list of words
most difficult for him to pronounce,
having him study these:
PEACH
SECRET
WHISPER
FINGERTIPS
FOREVER.

Edwin seems so happy
and contented
to be here with us

but startles whenever
the phone rings.
I pick it up.
I know she's on the other end—
nails that flash
with lacquer,
red like her hair.

I hang it up.
The children write words
for their daddy:

WHISPER
FINGERTIPS
FOREVER
SECRET.

To My Grandfather's Lover

Did the bullet have your name on it?
The imprint of your affair?
That night near the farmhouse
your body covering his
soft as geranium petals,
my grandmother's brittleness
breaking into fine kindling
to be set afire in your hands,
his kisses urgent,
his love
a blush that turned to blood.

Edwin's Brother

*I found Edwin
in a very bad condition*

*His speech has retarded quite a bit
in the last two weeks*

He was shot at a farmhouse
near Emporia,
fireflies
lit like constellations
in the air
spilling with kisses
nectar of honeysuckle
sweat along the crease of her neck
hands ripped
her silk slip
cream-colored,
inner petals of magnolia,
cicadas screeched,

nobody heard
her husband,

saw the gun flash
that night
nothing could keep them apart

*he is very nervous
breaks down
crying
quite a lot.*

Court

FOR MY GRANDMOTHER

Please be advised that Mrs. Harding
will be at the trial.
I shall thank you to also be present.

You wear your gray tweed
threaded with lavender,
smoky silk stockings,
sensible shoes.
Nothing too flashy.
The diamond ring, of course.
A little rouge.
No mascara,
no lipstick or maybe a touch
of mauve.

Let Mrs. Harlot paint herself
wear her flared skirt
her pink cloche hat
indiscrete perfume.

In the event
they put you on the witness stand
you will be asked
as to the age, height, and weight
of your husband
...and concerning
his present physical and mental state
all of which you are qualified to testify to
as you have seen him constantly
since he was injured.

You have been with him
teaching him slowly
to hold a cup
sip water.

Let *her* testify
how her husband clutched his .38,
crept through the grass
wet with sudden rain,
the hysteria of honeysuckle.

*I ask that you be there promptly
at 10 A.M.
I see no reason to have a summons
executed on you.
With kindest regard,*
        A.S. Harrison Jr.

I Imagine

Juror number eight:
*I certainly would have found him guilty
but that he owns the mortgage on my house.*

I imagine J.J. Harding—
hair thin, head thrown back,
I imagine
him clambering through a tangle
of clumped tubers, root balls,
I imagine him falling
climbing,
the sound of spring peepers rising,

his left hand holding right wrist to steady
the gun
silver   handle
aiming at Grandfather
between his eyes

his dark dancing eyes
spreading love over
his lover in her yellow dress

I imagine J.J. Harding
jaw clenched
eyes squinting in streams of sweat
folds of sweat in his neck
hand jerking   nearly missing

And the verdict crackles
and the verdict is:
NOT GUILTY

NOT GUILTY

Grandmother said after the trial:
I'm glad they didn't find him guilty
I would hate for my children to feel
they had put away a man for life

I imagine J.J. Harding
sipping a glass of buttermilk,
smoking a cigar.

Money

A widow, you held onto
what you could.
The cuckoo clock—
its chipped blue bird chirping the hours,
the corner cupboard
brimming
with majolica—
cherubs holding water lilies aloft
riding a froth of white waves.

Father McElroy's will
provided for you—a check each month.
Generous, but never enough.

Never the ease of
a long summer day,
and your mother still alive.

Another Ending

I wanted to take the bullet from your brain
give you another ending.
Or if you must be shot
I wanted your lover
to rush into your hospital room
and throw her body on yours—
a blanket of petals.

Neither happened.
Your wife brought you home,
your lover called,
the phone rang.
Paralyzed, you weren't able to answer
or maybe one time you did answer,
heard her sobbing
and you tried to speak Ls and Vs,
tried to seize love
from a shard of glass.

Blister

    I.

After Grandfather died,
she placed lilacs
in a milk glass bowl

painted her nails
pearl essence:
suitors began to call.

I don't think she was interested,
but enjoyed the attention.

In her parlor
I sat on my hands,
remembered my manners.

Take off your glasses, she whispered.

C.W., rumored Klansman, had blisters on his hands,
behind his back we called him *Blister.*

Would you like a praline?

At night lilacs
climbed the stairs.
Dogs strained at their chains,
barking.

    II.

I wore my plaid dress, Peter Pan collar,
kissed her rosewater cheek.

Out back, offered horses
sugar cubes
from lace doilies,
bit into a pear.

Blister laughed as
firebombs burst on TV.
In summer rain—the spray of bullets.
Clouds clog the wedge of his mouth
and a bouquet of death
came calling.

III.

Grandmother glints like steel
lightning in cotton gray clouds.

Blood floods into dreams—
a torrent of silence.

IV.

I'd just learned about sex
when *Blister* came calling.

I don't think they had it.
Something else
knit them together—

a hope chest of fear,
mothballs to keep it new.

CONTINUED

v.

Every summer
I entered the cage
of her love,

dreaming a circle of fire.

A field of stars
encircled us
as I rested my head
on her breast.

I want her to love me forever
but what would I do
for her love?
Skate out
over the black ice.

That Jew

A week after my husband's death, my daughter secretly married a Jewish boy

> From Grandmother's unsent letter to popular advice columnist, Dorothea Dix

You called my father "that Jew."
I hope they never have children

you told your friend, Janie Boes.
You loathed his loud voice,

legs crossed cowboy style.
Uncouth the way he picked his teeth

smoked cigars.
And why didn't he tell

his company
he was a Jew?

You wouldn't stoop so low
to haggle with a huckster,

a man who smelled money
when he met your daughter,

felt entitled to all that was hers.
At the corner store—

PEANUTS BAG YOUR OWN
10 CENTS—

he reached deep
into those burlap bags

and plundered.

Somehow

Somehow my grandmother
blotted out my Jewish name,
my hair curling
in her fingers,
nose that went on too long
like a bad story.

It allowed her to love me
in spite of the mistake;
my Scotch-Irish
to paint over
my Romanian Jew.

I got to be her favorite,
sit with her in the church pew,
listen to God
telling her she was right.

Gossip

Caught between her mother and mate
Mom took us each summer down South.

Sundays in white gloves,
we went to church,

grandmother in a black silk dress
ruched along the neck

locket of her dead son's and husband's hair
mixed in a gold breastpin.

Whispers in pews followed us
noisy with rustling taffeta.

What did they know?
Grandmother held her head high.

The fact that he's Jewish doesn't bother me in the least
Mom wrote to Grandmother from college.

And later: *You both have too much against
each other to ever be friends.*

Mom divided herself.
Up North she cooked the same Brunswick Stew—

chicken, corn, tomatoes, butter beans.
But it never tasted the same.

What I Forgot to Tell You After the Argument with My Father

I'm sorry you left
that cold November,
your stole gripping your shoulders.

Those beady eyes of dead minks
glaring
in the stiff dawn.

I wanted to run after you
but I was 4—my voice
frozen like first snowflakes.

You brought me a white
fur muff—
an early Christmas gift

and left your sorrow,
like the smell of black-veined pansies
we pressed in blue blotting paper.

Uncle

Robert Lemuel McElroy (August 21, 1929 - June 12, 1948) dropped dead unexpectedly at age eighteen.

I never met him.
He walked into my life
like his father—in a photo.
In his football uniform,
good looks like Grandfather—
ready to run with life
like a flag...then

June 1948—
Thalhimers Department Store—
a tuxedo under his arm,
ready to elope
with *that Catholic girl.*

All Petersburg turned out for his funeral
Grandmother leading the way,
spikes of red gladiolas
at the altar.

After they lowered his casket
she lingered over the grave:
*I'd rather see him dead
than married to that girl.*

Her Sister's Regrets
FOR MY GRANDMOTHER

After your mother died
Myrtle, your older sister,
became a stern tyrant.

No longer could you sit on the oak dresser,
stain your lips with red tissue paper

hike your skirt
and run in the blueberry field.

Your father sold everything, joined
the Seventh Day Adventists.

No smoking, no drinking. No smiling.
God always wore his capital letter.

You eloped, had two children,
but after your husband was shot,

your son
dropped dead.

Your sister wrote from her missionary
college her condolences:

God knows best
and you can rejoice that worse things

did not befall him.
The draft is just about to be passed.

There is no doubt
that we are on our way to the third world war.

I'm glad that if he had to pass
it was not on a blood-stained battlefield.

And, she added, *one more thing:*
It's hard for a mother without the help

of a father to guide a boy's steps
in these terrific days

with lures of evil on every side.
God knew it would be too difficult alone.

Caramel Cake, Burnt Sugar Icing

I.

After your mother died
the piano in the parlor fell silent,
doilies on polished wood gathered dust.

Gone were the caramel cakes
with burnt sugar icing,
peonies in milk glass bowls.

You were eleven
the winter morning your mother didn't come
to rub your hands in hers.

II.

Your father
sold his worldly goods,

put you in a boarding school
where they could make any child right-handed.

After graduation,
in your one pair of high laced-boots

you waited for the cicadas to die,
took a train to L.A.—

folded sheet of paper in your pocket
to McElroy's Real Estate Company.

You were hired—
a fellow southerner.

How was he to know
that you dreamed of lost gentility?

The hem of poverty
was sewn on every dress.

Grandfather became your suitor.
You served yellow cake,

rode horses among the Cacti,
fox-trotted at the Avalon Ballroom,

honeymooned on Catalina Island.
Blankets of stars fell on your nights together.

III.

We picnic in the cemetery
unwrapping our slices of caramel cake

You hand me plastic fork, napkin.
Your blue-veined hand untwists

the water jar. Thirsty, we drink
and sit. You brush a gold spider

from the box-elder, adjust
for each missing, a potted geranium.

Confederate Fantasy

*Honey, you know
we're related to Stonewall Jackson.*

Some say if Stonewall Jackson
had not been killed by friendly fire
the Confederates
would have won the war.
This would have worked
in your favor.
People would know their place,
something they were always forgetting.

You poured brandy
from a cut-glass decanter
on a table covered with green felt
where you played bridge
and told me about the great mine
that exploded
beneath the Confederates.
It was supposed to win the war. Instead
it filled your city
with casualties:
1,500 Confederates
3,798 Union.

Groundkeepers clear
the brown carpet
of pine needles
so the crater can still be seen—
170 feet long
60-80 feet wide
30 feet deep.
In Petersburg
you remind me
the Union was defeated.

You don't talk about
what came after:
Trapped on three sides
with a river to their back
the Confederates
made a suicidal last stand—
250 resisted 5000
as they climbed over
the fallen heaps of blue and gray.

The Ladies Memorial Association—
oldest continuous women's organization
in the United States—
decorates graves each Memorial Day
on May 30th
and June 9th for the 30,000 plus Confederate soldiers
buried at Blandford Cemetery.

You only celebrate one day.

We Sat Every Night

We sat every night, watched the news
as Freedom Riders boarded buses
in your home state,
traveled to Montgomery, Birmingham.

I was eleven:
*The government says colored people can vote, Nana,
why are these whites against it?*

You:
*People up North are always criticizing us southerners
but the colored are still treated
with more respect here
than most anywhere else.*

Pictures of a scorched bus, people choking
by the side of the road.
Where is that 'anywhere else'?

When I argued with you
you chalked it up to my tainted Jewish blood—
something I couldn't help.

I imagined Freedom Riders
pulling into our town.
I'd run out like Janie Miller

the 12-year-old white girl
who lugged five-gallon buckets of water
to those gasping by the side of their firebombed bus
as her neighbors cheered:
Let them burn!

But was I too chicken to have my family
run out of town like Janie's?

*Honey, these riots have not equaled the violence
in other places.*

Janie changed schools, hid the newspaper photo of herself
showing an act of kindness,
heart's voice muffled for generations.

You rose to fix me another slice of pecan pie
the way we liked it — warm
vanilla ice cream melting on top.

Nana, where are those 'other places'?

But my words are leaves
whirling on your patio.

Not Much Different

Roger Couch and Goober Lewallyn
weren't much different than your neighbors—
fresh-faced young men
that said *Yesum* and bowed their heads in church.
They wanted to be heroes like many young men,
saw their chances as the mob pushed forward.
Goober had gathered a fistful of rags,
Couch grabbed the can of kerosene
Oh my God, they're going to burn us up—
screams from inside the bus.
Sounds far off, caught in clouds.
When Couch threw the fisted knot of flames
it rose like a football tossed downfield,
within seconds exploded,
sending gray smoke throughout the bus.
And that night they were hoisted aloft,
paraded and praised
in a wild tumult of victory.

Fear is a Face Without Features

Blurred faces of the mob
pushed up against bus windows
kerosene-soaked rags in hands
metal pipes gripped;
did tragedy bring them
to this desolate place,
was it their mother's milk? Father's hate?
My grandmother, her jaw set,
could be one of these women,
some carrying children.
Mothers yelling *Burn them alive!*

When did I stop being one of these children?

Everything is changing, I say.
It will be better.
She blinks at birds fighting
beneath the chinaberry tree, blue feathers
litter the stone walkway.
It's time to water the geraniums
out at the cemetery.

Fear is a face without features.

Trash

Frederick Douglass escaped slavery and was amazed to see white men up north wealthy without slaves. Down south, poor whites who had no slaves were known as poor white trash.

Imprinted in my DNA
the time your father sold everything —
your beautiful belongings
taken away in a horse-drawn cart,
thrown out like trash.

Like you I feared poverty.
Born in a different age
I would have clambered
not to be destitute —
a woman with mended stockings or
no stockings at all.
I like to think I wouldn't have acquiesced
two hundred years ago,
wouldn't have followed you to the slave auctions,
kept my head down as you haggled prices,
as now you haggle with the antique dealer
over Chippendale chairs
covered with elaborate crewel work
of silver and lapis birds.

With Grandmother at My Mother's Funeral

In your black silk suit
white hair a halo

in late May sun
you slide into

J.T. Morris's
hearse.

Later we stand over Mom's
new-cut grave.

Too many mums
you say.

You know the way
a plot should be kept.

We've been coming for years
watering the potted geraniums

with a battered teapot.
We sit on the stone bench.

In the box-elder a spider rustles.
I'm so glad, you say,

*to have my family
all together again.*

Food and Flowers, Memorial

The Board of the Petersburg Home for Ladies (Gloxinia)

Mrs. Bessie Callender (pink and white roses)

Miss. Nellie Stables at Kings (Pink Carnations)

Whitmore's restaurant (a beautiful tray of food)

Sadie Marion (red sweetheart roses from their garden)

Crater Ridge Boys (White Callas with Yellow Majestic Daisies)

Mrs. Bain (pansies and delicious pecan pie)

Major Horver (12 beautiful yellow roses)

Miss Mabel, Lucy Webb, and Brother (Cake and Pudding) (sweetheart roses)

Mrs. Alice Savory (Cross of white carnations or mums, red roses and ribbon)

Mrs. R. A. Printemp (arrangement white Callas with yellow Majestic Daisies)

Mr. Lavenstein (Standing spray of yellow Mums)

Virginia Perkins (a book of verses)

Mrs. Robert Lawrence (Large tray of sliced ham)

Reverend Paige (fruitcake with green cherries)

You Forgive Them

Your husband, then both children tried to escape.
They lie here beneath red dirt
that drank the blood
of your *Confederate boys*.
All opening their mouths wide
to your battered teapot
as you water their graves,
forgive them for leaving you.

III

Stories

Why do the dead keep
telling us stories,
insistent,
keeping us up at night,
nudging us when we pass cemeteries?
We think we escape them
but they know how to return,
to creep into the cedar waxwing's shrill cry,
flutter up under the breast bone
when lavender spills into twilight.
We try to go on,
to pretend we don't hear them
chattering in the corner—
as ghosts come
to brush our hair.

Affairs Run in the Family
FOR MY MOTHER

He had an affair,
your father.
Did she ensnare
or did he lure

her to the farm
tangled with stars,
honeysuckle? An alarm,
a shot mars

your father in an instant,
his life collapsed
from that moment. It won't
ever be the same. Soul lapsed.

Like the bullet in his brain
the affair was embedded —
a tombstone wet with rain —
in your memory. Your fears, leaded,

marched toward
your own husband's ten-year
secret. And just as your mother would hoard
evidence — cinnamon, tear-

stained letters — you found a picture
of Arizona though he said
he went to Akron. (So sure
he brought a souvenir.) You made

excuses as, year after year, signs
gathered in a box of rosewood
which one day, I,
your daughter, find.

Vacation Photo

FOR MY FATHER

In the vacation photo you sit
at the head of the table—
tan, smiling—it is

just before your ten-year affair.
We cluster around you
your cufflinks clinquant in night's salt air.

We are about to devour crab cakes, red snapper.
Mother's small teeth are pearls
glistening beneath tear-drop lights,

my two brothers eager
in madras sports jackets smile
just before your affair.

Could life have continued
incandescent
as the glow from your cigarette?

I am hunched in red taffeta
headed towards my nervous breakdown
just before your affair

and mother seems unaware
a mystery
will leave her dead at forty-eight

nor does my oldest brother
sitting before baked potato aglow in tinfoil
see cancer looming.

In the vacation photo the table gathers secrets
splayed on pink linen.
      Forgiveness glitters along the hem.

Samplar: Betrayal

FOR MY MOTHER AND GRANDMOTHER

You've pitched your tents
in my blood and I want you gone.
No longer a fragile thing who dents
when brushed or bruised, I've drawn

a different course from you.
I wouldn't seek it
though I can withstand betrayal. True,
you gave me the split

bullet in grandfather's brain
but half that shot passed through
as I passed through your pain
to the place where love drew

a picture and the dead
are stormless now. Where goldwork trims
everything and in the thread
of a needle love spins.

After

FOR MY MOTHER

After your funeral
we eat biscuits and chocolate.
I watch birds fall
from the sky in arcs and shake

their wings in the dying sun.
Vireo, thrush, cedar waxwing.
The magnolias have just begun
to spread pink gauze over the deepening

green, as your face returns
in luster of dark wood:
a young woman, you spurned
the only man your mother said you could

marry. Offered your smile
that lit everything to those who
kept it, and to those who tried
and could not. Like me, who

(caught, consumed
into myself), went away
and in your lifetime turned.
I see you here today

as if you were alive,
as if your hands could still unleash
those gifts, those wild
birds, those words never released

in your lifetime, which strive
in me to take voice, as I listen.
For the dead leave and we spend our lives
learning to speak with them.

Escape

Some said you were cursed.
The cemetery became your second home.

Turn left on Magnolia Lane, stop
when you see the crypt; if you continue

you'll see Old Blandford Church,
its Tiffany windows radiant as gems.

Over there the Crater where your *Boys*
nearly won the war. You were my escape

from a father whose fist came down
on glass tables shattering everything.

You were my refuge, my devoted one,
though I eschewed your fears.

When did I begin to wonder how other water tasted?
You yanked me back that day, my pigtails flying:

You know better! Read the sign, Whites Only.
Did I ever know better?

We don't choose who we're born to.
And do we really choose who we love?

You and Stonewall Jackson

I wondered if being related to Stonewall Jackson
was like the Chippendale chairs that turned out

to be knockoffs, or the *antique* highboy,
circa 1967.

But he had the same high forehead
and straight nose as you,

the same firm jaw;
his set on the "lost cause" of the Confederacy.

Better to fight for a lost cause
that is noble, you once said.

I wondered,
brushing off spider webs

from crepe myrtle
the color of blushing cheeks

as we sat at the cemetery
on those hot afternoons,

if you felt life had been
a noble lost cause.

But no, you'd rewritten everything.
Stonewall Jackson was considered

the greatest tactical commander of the civil war
and you arranged your life

the way you dreamed it.
Your husband never had an affair.

He was shot by some lunatic
and you nursed him patiently for years.

We pulled up the weeds
near everyone's headstone

watered the geraniums
and went home.

Of Jackson you said:
In death he became an icon.

Talking

I taped your voice once.
When I play it
I smell tincture of peppermint

you swabbed in dressers,
rosewater splashed
on your wrinkled face.

Your voice is strong,
with a hint
of girlish laughter

then I ask you about
your father;
you pause.

In the background
birds trill.
Crickets loud at the end of summer.

*Father was awfully strict
especially to my younger brother Bill.
He tied him up once to a tree*

*and whipped him something awful.
I still remember
those switchings on his back.*

And you? I ask.   No answer.
I reach to stop the tape.
Far off dogs bay.

The Last Time I See Her

I pick her up from the nursing home
drive to King's Barbecue out on the highway.

I know I know you, she says
but she doesn't remember my name.

I want my old grandmother back.
The one who grumbles when the waitress is slow.

The whites of her eyes
cloud with confusion.

Do you like your new home I ask.
It's not my home she says — suddenly lucid, bitter.

*Take me back to my home
don't tell them they'll never find out.*

I can't do that, I say.
I don't say: Your home is gone —

your cuckoo clock
with its painted blue bird

cooing
in my apartment up North.

Her hand
grips my arm.

CONTINUED

Coleslaw, barbecue sandwiches
dripping with sauce, rescue me.

We eat in silence. No old people here.
Miss Nellie, her favorite waitress,

is out. There's no one to help me
put her mind back together.

I drive back
along South Crater Road

afraid she'll suddenly
grab the steering wheel.

I don't want to go to the cemetery
with her under a headstone.

At the nursing home
I kiss her wrinkled cheek: *Goodbye*.

Outside, in the field,
there are no fireflies.

Meditations on Death

Sound of rain,
sweetness of peaches
smashed on the red earth.
She dabs creases
with tincture of rosewater,
petals fall
into a grave
waiting for them.

*

Cedar waxwing's
trill in pear trees,
smell of lemon wax
on the stairs.
You keep watch
by the grave fresh cut.

*

Eiderdown quilt
whooshes —
dust motes
like pinpoints of memory
settle on your cedar chest,
a stencil of green and rust
partridges.

Perpetual Care

Dear Laura Sue,
In my lock box at the Bank of Virginia
is my receipt for the cemetery square.
After I die, there is room for one more burial.

Will I lie in the red earth beside you
where all hurt and betrayal vanish
below the towering magnolia
the smell of boxwoods and fresh dirt?

Also the receipt for perpetual care.
If our plot is not kept up
please, take the receipt and see about it.

Who will care for you perpetually?

I return to this place
                              where the dead lie
    spilling secrets.

On the polished headstones
                I trace my finger over their names.

Together

Crocheted doilies
stretched to lace cobwebs
on your mahogany table
we eat our Spanish crème and trifle
laugh as we always did
as if no one ever left anyone.

Though our dead lie
flat as tin cutouts
knocked down at an amusement arcade,

here we are,
by the walnut bookcase near the fire,

and no one is missing.

Shot In The Head

2017

LEE VARON

FIRST PLACE ♦ POETRY COLLECTION

LEE VARON IS A SOCIAL WORKER IN THE BOSTON area. She was born in Chicago and grew up in Illinois. As a child, many of her summers were spent with her maternal grandmother in Petersburg, Virginia.

In addition to poetry, Varon also writes prose and won the 2015 *Briar Cliff Review* Fiction Award. Her poetry has been nominated for a Pushcart Prize and has been published in various literary journals, including *Atlanta Review*, *Ibbetson Street*, *Euphony*, *Tampa Review*, *Inscape*, *Westview*, *The Somerville Times*, *Wilderness House Literary Review*, *Muddy River Poetry Review*, and *Oddball Magazine*.

ALSO BY LEE VARON

Spare Change News Poems: An Anthology by Homeless People and Those Touched by Homelessness
Edited by Lee Varon and Marc Goldfinger
IBBETSON STREET PRESS, 2018

Affairs Run in the Family
FINISHING LINE PRESS, 2017

Adopting On Your Own: The Complete Guide to Adopting as a Single Parent
FARRAR, STRAUS AND GIROUX, 2000

THE FUTURE IS UP FOR GRABS, CONCEIVED BY THE IMAGINATION, CONSTRUCTED WITH WORDS, AND EXPLAINED AS A STORY.

SUNSHOT PRESS

— FIRST PLACE WINNER —
2017 SUNSHOT BOOK AWARD™ FOR FICTION

Bloodshot Stories
by Jeff P. Jones

You want it darker? Jeff P. Jones carries on in the trajectory that runs from Kafka through Philip K. Dick to Cormac McCarthy (with a sprinkling of John Barth thrown in). Whether inviting the reader to comb through the dank stacks of a Stalin archive, or sweat inside the soldered-closed cab of a post-apocalyptic dump truck, or become an atom splitting from the inside, or a single brain dispersing into the universe — these brilliantly researched and deeply imagined stories are never the expected. A stunning collection.

—**Janet Burroway**
Author of *Writing Fiction: A Guide to Narrative Craft* (9th edition)

SUNSHOT PRESS

2017 SUNSHOT BOOK PRIZE™ FOR NONFICTION

Human Rights and Wrongs
Reluctant Heroes Fight Tyranny
by Adrianne Aron

A clever joker once said, 'I dream of a world where chickens can cross the road without having their motives questioned.' I, as a mental health professional, dream of one where psychologists will understand why Ernesto Cruz drinks himself into a stupor, why Eva refuses to speak about what happened to her in Honduras, why Mrs. Malek is afraid to return to Afghanistan. In a collection of serious yet entertaining human interest stories, Adrianne Aron's Human Rights and Wrongs *engages the general reader while inspiring psychologists to think outside the box.*

— Shawn Corne, Ph.D.
Clinical Psychologist, Albany, California

SUNSHOT PRESS

2017 SUNSHOT BOOK PRIZE™ FOR FICTION

An Incomplete List of My Wishes

by Jendi Reiter

Jendi Reiter is a masterful short story writer. Truth and humor are woven intricately, ripe with emotion and stripped down to the bone. You will read these again and again.

—Jacqueline Sheehan

New York Times bestselling author of Lost and Found (William Morrow) and The Tiger in the House (Kensington)

SUNSHOT PRESS

SUNSHOT PRESS WOULD NOT HAVE BEEN POSSIBLE WITHOUT
THE BOLD SUPPORT OF THE FOLLOWING POETS & WRITERS:

Barbara A.   Adrianne A.   T. A.   David A.   Idris A.   Kaye A.   Thomas J.   Paul M.
Samantha T.   Linda F.   Craig O.   Gary P.   LeeAnn P.   Brian P.   Gary P.   T. M.
Ron V.   Marina H.   Eric W.   Sandra W.   Stuart W.   Emma W.   Fred W.
Rebecca L.   Barbara D.   Dana C.   Elaine C.   Kristen C.   Patricia B.
Timothy W.   James W.   Cynthia W.   Fred W.   Jeanne W.   Lee V.
Benjamin B.   Claire B.   Jerome   Marge B.   Patricia B.   Ruth M.
Barbara S.   Rachel B.   Ellen A.   Patricia R.   Nancy R.   Vincent J.
Alfred M.   Gregory S.   Jan S.   Catherine S.   James S.   Harvey S.
Lisa P.   Luke W.   Leland J.   Gail W.   Lillo W.   Pam W.   Lyzette W.
Terri M.   Sean M.   Deana N.   Jed M.   Barbra N.   Joel N.   Paul N.
Mara S.   Ramon B.   Bruce R.   John R.   Jendi R.   Paddy R.   Susan P.
Stanley R.   Andrew S.   Lynn S.   Kathryn P.   Anneliese S.   Mick S.
Lones S.   Corey M.   Richard S.   Nathan S.   Andrew S.   Elaine S.
J.D. B.   Roberta D.   Susan S.   Victoria S.   Joanne S.   Jen S.
Felix N.   Evelyn V.   Derek U.   Mike T.   Naomi M.   Jayshiro T.
Simone M.   Aida Z.   Cindy Z.   Paula Z.   Allan Y.   Felice W.
Tori M.   Karen H.   Ken M.   Barbara M.   Matt M.   Sean M.
Anca H.   David H.   Dennis H.   Eileen H.   Linda H.   W. H.
Kate H.   Jack H.   Roberta H.   Eunice H.   Nancy H.
Jonathan G.   Bruce G.   Joshua B.   Thomas B.   Catherine B.   Enid H.
Susan C.   Danny C.   Laurie C.   Julius C.   Richard B.   R.C. G.   Adam G.
Casey C.   Garry C.   LaRue C.   Bob R.   Kathy C.   Susan C.   Margo B.
Rusty D.   Effie D.   Deborah D.   Annie D.   Howard G.
Bill G.   Tina G.   Nina G.   Paula F.   Jon F.
Jerri B.   Kathryn C.   Robynn C.   Greer G.
William E.   Mary D.   Frank D.   George D.
Ruth F.   Benjamin F.   Teressa E.   Renato E.
Chad F.   Andrew H.   Ann H.   Lorien H.   Jeff J.   Martin I.   Mark H.
Christina F.   Ellen L.   John L.   David L.   Djelloul M.   Bernard M.
Richard L.   Jeffrey M.   Kevin M.   Peter M.   Wendell M.   Clif M.
Genese G.   Howard E.   Alison L.   Kurt L.   Naomi L.   Sam L.
Albert L.   Patricia B.   Chad B.   Mark B.   David B.   Julia L.
Roberta G.   Olaf K.   Kristie L.   Jacqueline L.   Lee L.   Thom K.
Joanne G.   Francis J.   Joyce K.   Marylou S.   Peter K.
James C.   Jason H.   Ryan H.   Georganne H.   Cleda H.
Joan C.   Edie C.
Leslee B.
Beth C.
Jackie M.

THANK YOU

SUNSHOTS.ORG

SUNSHOT PRESS

www.ingramcontent.com/pod-product-compliance
Lightning Source LLC
Chambersburg PA
CBHW020145130526
44591CB00030B/235